Contents

WHAT'S WRONG?

If you have diabetes, it can
make you feel tired and unwell.
You may feel very thirsty a lot
of the time. Sometimes you run
out of energy, look pale and
feel dizzy or shaky. You may
often get stomach aches or
headaches too.

Did you know?

There are two types
of diabetes.
Children mostly
have type 1.

Han's story

At first, I didn't know what was wrong. I just felt tired and thirsty all the time. The doctors did some tests. They found out I have type 1 diabetes.

WHAT'S GOING ON?

If you have type 1 diabetes, your body does not make enough **insulin**. This is a chemical that helps you turn the sugar you eat into energy. Without it, your body doesn't get enough energy, so you feel tired. You burn **muscle** or **fat** for energy instead, so you lose weight.

Dear Doc

Why does diabetes make you thirsty?

Extra sugar in your blood makes you go to the toilet more often, so you feel more thirsty.

8

Did you know?

Insulin is made in the body by the *pancreas*, which also makes juices that help you digest food.

INSULIN INJECTIONS

If you have type 1 diabetes, you need to have insulin **injections** every day. A special pen is used to inject the insulin into your arm, leg or belly. Some people with type 2 diabetes need to inject insulin too. Others take pills, or control their diabetes with what they eat or drink.

Did you know?

Some people use pumps or *inhalers* to take insulin.

William's story

Dad used to give me my insulin injections but now I've learnt to do them myself. I'm quite used to them, so I don't mind too much.

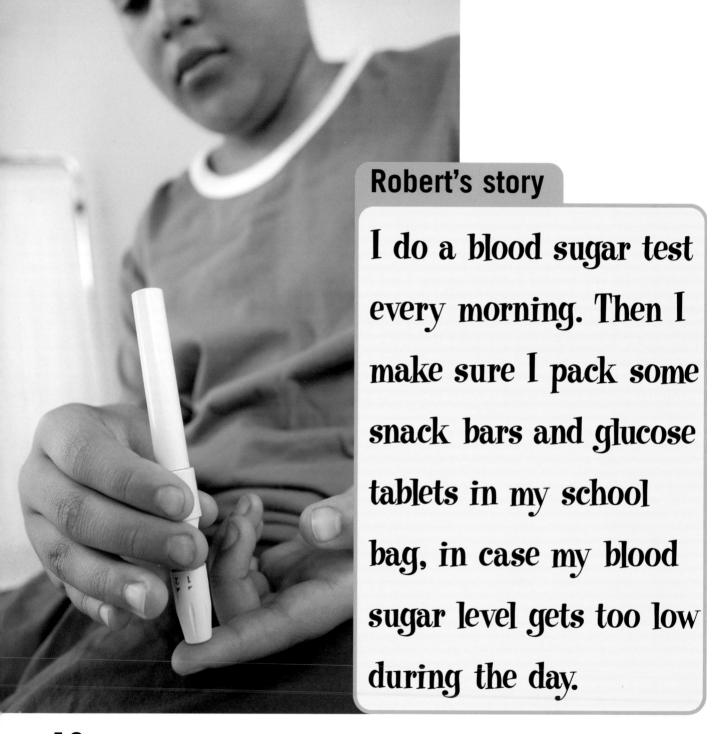

Robert's story

I do a blood sugar test every morning. Then I make sure I pack some snack bars and glucose tablets in my school bag, in case my blood sugar level gets too low during the day.

BLOOD SUGAR TESTS

When you have diabetes, you may need to do **blood sugar tests** every day. Sometimes, if you have had too much insulin, your **blood sugar level** can fall too low. You can then look pale and feel dizzy and shaky. This is called having a **'hypo'**. When this happens, you need to have a snack to give you energy.

Dear Doc

What is a blood sugar test?

It is a simple test where you prick your finger and squeeze a drop of blood onto a test paper.

TYPE 2 DIABETES

Type 2 diabetes usually affects older people. If you have this type of diabetes, the cells in your body do not use insulin properly. Sugar from your food can stay in your blood, so your blood sugar level becomes too high. This can make you feel tired and unwell. Like type 1 diabetes, your blood sugar can also sometimes get too low.

Did you know?

Type 2 diabetes can run in families.

14

Dear Doc

What causes type 2 diabetes?

The risk of getting it is higher if you eat too much sugary food, like biscuits, are overweight and don't exercise enough.

DIET AND DIABETES

When you have diabetes, it is important to eat a healthy **diet**. You should try to eat plenty of **whole grain** foods and fresh fruit and vegetables. It is important not to eat too many sweets, sugary foods or drinks as your blood sugar level may become too high.

Did you know?
Foods like baked beans, ketchup and sausages can all contain sugar.

When mum goes shopping, she checks amounts of sugar on food labels. I can have treats sometimes, but I usually eat lots of healthy foods!

17

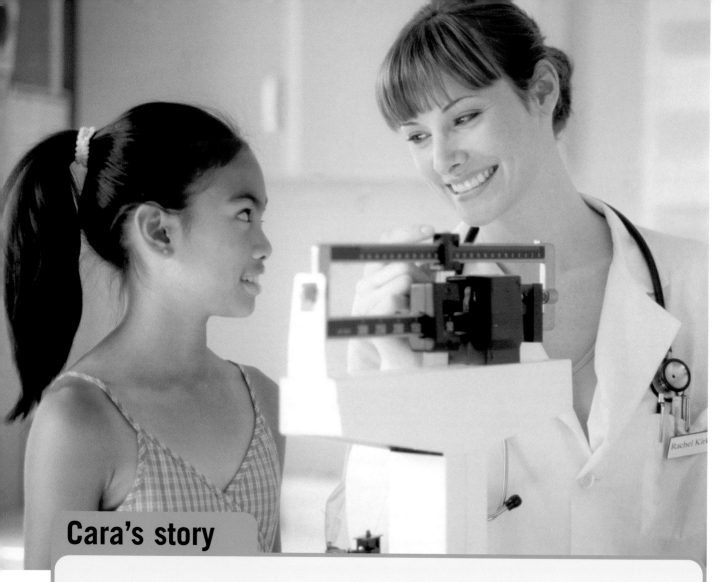

Cara's story

I don't mind going for my check-ups. I know the doctor and she is always nice to me.

CHECK-UPS

If you have diabetes, you need to have regular check-ups with a doctor or nurse. They weigh and measure you to see how well you are growing. They look through your blood sugar results and advise you on diet and exercise.

Dear Doc

Why are diet and exercise so important?

Because they help you to control your blood sugar levels and stay a healthy weight.

LIVING WITH DIABETES

When you have diabetes, you should tell your teachers and friends so they can help if you feel unwell. It is important to take care of your health by eating a healthy diet and getting plenty of exercise. Exercise will help your body use insulin and keep you fit.

20

Dear Doc

What makes blood sugar levels go up or down?

Food, exercise, growing and stress all affect blood sugar levels.

Becky's story

I wear a **medic-alert** bracelet. It tells people I have diabetes. If I felt hypo someone could ring the number to get help for me.

Glossary

Blood sugar level   the amount of sugar carried in someone's blood

Blood sugar tests   testing a drop of blood for sugar levels

Diet   the food that someone generally eats

Fat   tissue in the body that stores energy, protects the bones and keeps someone warm

Hypo   (hypoglycaemic) how someone feels when their blood sugar is too low

Inhaler   a device for breathing in medicine

Injection   using a needle or a special pen to put something into the blood

Insulin   a chemical made in the body that controls the amount of sugar in the blood

Medic-alert   a medical warning worn on the body

Muscle   tissue in the body that we use to make movements

Pancreas   a part of the body that makes insulin and other chemicals it needs

Whole grains   rice and cereal grains like wheat and oatmeal that still have their outer husk and fibre (roughage)